SplitLevel Texts

the TREATMENT of MONUMENTS

Alan
GILBERT

SplitLevel Texts
Ann Arbor, MI 48103
http://www.splitleveltexts.com

Copyright © 2012 by Alan Gilbert
Printed in the United States of America
Cover design by Melissa Dettloff / hoorayforever.org
Cover image: Seher Shah
Unit Object (bent) [detail]
Graphite and gouache on paper
22 x 30 inches, 56 x 72 cm, 2001

Interior design by Monique Grimord / moniquegrimord.org
ISBN: 978-0-9858111-0-5

Library of Congress Control Number: 2012948708

the TREATMENT *of* MONUMENTS

CONTENTS

RELATIVE HEAT INDEX

1)

Clowns are always
in a box.

Every child is first abandoned
before the law.

The clinking links
of a thick metal chain
run quickly through a pulley.

     Nothing is gathered up.

     Nothing finds its way home.

Styrofoam mackerels swirl
in a flooded railway yard,

       where blind conductors perform

       from a soggy script.

2)

Both the cows and the pasture are engineered for efficiency.

The camera attaches to a gun turret,

just as looking at a light
doesn't always reveal its source

     or its substitute for memory.

I found the hair dryer's design practical, ergonomic.

     Days tumble to the bottom corner
     of a tattered calendar. Words
     jostle and blur on the page.

This fire is not cleansing.

It overloads the circuits,
their fissures, and other
rooms to roam
     on a feedback tundra.

3)

Everything is capable of being broken.

The mast of a miniature ship
snaps off beneath a fountain's cascade.
Children are silenced by a desert

where steel shimmers in the heat.

Who called? What's the address?

You hand me slivers.
You hand me over.

Storm clouds gather west of the west.
Slumming time.

4)

What are the conditions of knowledge?
How is knowledge conditioned?

Does the spoon get placed inside the knife?

Disassembling the architecture
to the hum of machines and electronics,
next door to an impregnable bank
staffed by young women wearing
large engagement rings.

Rubbing the eyes until a dull sheen develops,
as individual trademarks form
a universal language
piped into
an elevator full of galley slaves
rhythmically mimicking a long pull on the oars

while wearing silver mittens.

I got biscuits.

5)

I don't need to be disciplined any more.

A brisk wind bends
the landscape blue,
where a train never
arrives on time,
out beyond the station
of the present's passing.

diverse   divested

Past the arteries of commerce,
   the roadside scenic vistas,
   the geographical markers,
   the easy-off/easy-on fast food restaurants,
   the vast migrations and reverse migrations,
   the burning trash in the distance,
   the rest areas,
   the ubiquitous warm night crickets.

All of it dark with history.

6)

Car exhaust and soot gradually turn
the public Christmas ornaments gray
where they hang from stoplights and lampposts
like a small-town 4th of July parade.

Wrapping a wounded TV with gauze and medical tape.

this word as word   that word as word
                inserted opaque and transparent
          perambulating yet crowding the airwaves

It wasn't true.

Decaying food slowly accumulated in the refrigerator.
B-movie zombies ate our brains, anyway;
and then used a Zamboni to make their escape,

        just as this page is taking too long to download.

I'm a big plastic bucket full of frogs at the market.

        Waiting for response . . . Waiting for reply . . .

7)

Where would you be without love?

Happy to lean against desire.

Information is not innocent, either.

Please bring the car around;
then watch the clowns spill out.

(After a certain point, I stopped counting.)

(I've stopped.)

(Stopped.)

Who's going to stop it?

8)

All beginnings are endings:

       some blue like tissue pulled from the box,

       some red like flesh torn from the bone.

starred   elusive

A TV mumbles through the floorboards.

       An athlete appears on a cereal box placed
       in a television show made into a movie
       with a soundtrack by a singer who wears
       the athlete's jersey in a video.

       I read about the athlete, ate the cereal,
       watched the television show, missed
       the movie, heard the song, didn't buy
       the CD, but checked out the video.

Poetry is not entirely unhappy
with its debasement.

The window's wide-screen projection
folded itself into an endless swollen summer.
Green sparks squirt where chips of time scatter.

There are good reasons to be suspicious of beauty.

16

9)

Readers are not fish to hook.
A knot eventually shakes loose.

A crack ran horizontally across the whole windshield,
trapping the light in quick glimpses.

History's ellipsis
provides ephemeral names for highways.
Now, every trucker I see
reminds me of you, mom.

sidetrack   backtrack   bushwhack

A lawn burns black
around a house built of bones
in the valley of cancer.

10)

How did it get to be called public opinion?

Asking:
>   Who tracks the prehistoric flight paths of pterodactyls over
>   New Jersey?
>   Who knows what it's like to be a girl?

On certain days, you can see all the way back
to a billboard behind childhood.

Unaccompany me.

>   Memory
>   rewrites
>   history
>   as
>   history
>   rewrites
>   memory.

>   All art
>   so far
>   occurs during
>   wartime.

11)

An economy before the gold rush
sweats the consequences,
puts in a railroad line,
and awaits the inevitable gamblers,
                    the samplers,
                        and the romantics,
            with their decibels and old coins.

            Fire in the city and
                dry lightning on the plains
flash neon in front of history's gloomy hotel

that staggers along with an emptied revolver
in its pale hand.

It can't be rebuilt,
no matter how many celebrities smile and offer to pitch in.

Instead,
            construct elaborate stage sets.

12)

Channel-surfing through the sitcoms
to get to another commercial.

A professional driver on a closed course
crashed into a camera mount.

There are many angles to choose from,
each with obstructed views.

I bobbed along for days
and ended up where I started.

The porch light remained obscure
and a car still idled out front.

All the draft dodgers now want to make war,
propping up a ladder that extends to nowhere—

      the small space of silence between the cricket's leg and wing
      where Apache helicopters bring the stuttering news.

13)

A drink cart accidentally overturned
while the plane taxied,
triggering the inflatable escape slides.
Dogs howled in the cargo hold
as their owners slid by.

It's impossible to tell where the river ends and the ocean begins.
Garbage barges break the water's smooth surface.

How much force can a building withstand?
What power does knowledge confirm or deny?

Seat cushions may be used as flotation devices
in the event of an emergency water landing.

A sudden storm eager to reach its destination
ignored the traffic signals synchronized on a grid.
In the morning, workers were already repairing the roof.

Sometimes love presses down hard.

You can take away the father.

Reprise the role.
Revise the rule.

14)

A virtual weather map plots
geography in a digital expanse
of history's frequent wardrobe changes
filmed through a green glass bottle
washed up on shore
where the dark imperium gathers its troops.

Cities shift their concrete features.
The local flora changes its hue.
An irradiated lake glows genially
at twilight,

as bathers splash around its soft, sandy edges.

The self makes stupid;
most silence is not profound.
A small pile of bricks waits to be made
into a cash register that also bakes pizzas.

Rain slickens the pavement outside,
and wheels lose a little of their grip on the surface.

15)

Fiction binds throughout the day
and surrounds the manor house with torches

that also reflect in an office building's
revolving glass doors,
                        the dirty windows,

        just as a serial poem never starts over.

A streetlamp patchwork of glittering shadows
paves a take-out window's S-curve
                        hot asphalt

                for the drive-thru soul.

The street quiets down
after a garbage truck hauls off the page.

                Then another one
[repeat]
        takes its place.

16)

A meteorologist eats his way forward

to the sound of an electric can opener
and an out-of-tune piano,

the rain *ping ping ping* against a tin roof.

A concrete retaining wall
sags in the wet earth,
                              splattering mud sunspots

                    spun from a dentist's vinyl chair.

The next wave is Pepsi's advertising campaign.

          Look for big branded pandas to float across a gray sky
          or encircle a school of submerged dorsals.

17)

Phantom limbs close the ivory lid
on a nation's looped lullabies.

Temporal hamhocks thaw
amid a swirl of global sands
that jams the guns of empire
lost and regained.

A voice stuffed with glass
is a claim against lore—

laying a tongue on the tracks,

laying tracks on the tongue.

There's an uninvited guest
called hope who lounges
on the couch watching TV all day
and eats the remaining food
in a refrigerator

that's periodically lapped by a rippling wake.

18)

Who's left picking up the check
written on a doctor's messy prescription pad
that transcribes the daily negotiations with power—

      (codename: Robin Banks)

—an atomic drift into oncoming traffic
from McDonald's to the mall?

Billboards clustered on a commuter highway
topple like dominos.

That nurse has handcuffs and a knife.

      The rest is rendered irrelevant   inconsequential,

which is different from just vanishing
into the world.

19)

History is a constant ringing in the ears
like locating a house in a tornado
with stars outlined in pink marker
unfixed in the sky above.

Exhaust fumes make palm trees jiggle
in the distance.
Voices inaudibly argue
on the other side of bulletproof glass.

stamped   branded

I remember planned obsolescence:

      the shoddy paint job,

      the bad haircut,

      the kitchen sink full of dirty dishes.

          An x-ray peers through

   a defective heart

             glowing on a barium screen.

20)

winter sun ~~reptile museum~~

A winter sun in the reptile museum

      totes Budweiser in a rubber cooler

and gets plastered with metaphor
          or culture.

What's natural?

Long gone past literal.

Poetry's images slip,
because I'm all wet.

21)

This isn't a jam band; it's a dance band.

Illiteracy is a discourse.

The radiator only heats the front half of the room.

The car bomb's engine was found on a nearby balcony.

Any questions?

Famous is a relative category.

The blood flow stops once the wound begins to close.

Please check server.

Antelope twitch their ears at a saltlick.

What are the five things you can't live without?

A dog rears back on its haunches.

It seems, EKG, as if you must have a strong heart, too.

Satellites photograph license plates from space.

Nice to meet you.

Defective O-rings were not the sole cause of the explosion.

22)

A cracked ruler takes time's malic measure
in a submarine built for one
with salad bar and dim searchlight included.

Marvelous aquatic creatures push their phosphorescent snouts
up against the compression-resistant glass
to relieve the tedium of seafloor dark and cold.

Insomnia's foundling skull lurches into the night,
as the fatal vessel methodically chugs along
in its quest for myth and dollars.

23)

The plastic needle drops below empty,
with no gas station around for miles,

     and its punch in the face,

     its boot on the neck of the producers.

There's no music in the desert,
except the contrails of jets.

     Literal
     crow's nest;
     literal
     widow.

The burgundy gleam
of an oil well's rusty lure

lies face down in the snow.

MORE MORPHINE

After the storm and before the storm, the air hums
with the sounds of TVs and radios. Long-time listener,
first-time caller—with a mouthful of static. A switchboard
lights up in flashing yellow, as a transmission crackles
in the dark atmosphere. A newsreel showed the winter siege
in 3-D, with snow falling between gun turrets pivoting
toward a target located right behind an audience ducking
in a curled wave. While I appreciate the need for safety,
I'm not so sure about pulling the seatbelt tight across
your neck. The refreshment stand stays open after the credits roll.
A fire exit sign shines faintly over the door.

What began as a friendly game of cards ended with me
losing my shirt and a prosthetic leg. Oh, dirty, dirty disco!
We float in a murky motel pool where a whale's eye
is still smaller than an inflatable dinghy. Every grafted fiction
tells its fractured stories, including the ones inseparable
from flesh or packed in dry ice and rushed by helicopter
to the hospital. Thin doors flap as first feet, then guts,
and finally the head come hurtling through on a gurney,
with images viewed on a beige monitor by the attending
nurse and physician.

I discovered that fishing with a piece of cheese tied to a string
won't impress the experts dressed in Gore-Tex. Language
is an ongoing negotiation. War keeps retired generals busy,
bombing videotaped rocks into videotaped sand, or the tip
of a knife moves slightly faster than the hand that wields it.
A city's midnight luster illuminates the sky for miles, rowing
an enormous galleon into surrounding farms that unfurl beneath
a cropduster's misted wings swooping low over various species
of roadkill. Life gets messy along the way. It gets flattened out,

and spills over the edges, as in the story about the aboveground
swimming pool and the cinderblock chicken coop.
First it was spring, then it was summer, then it was winter—
no, that's not right!—then it was fall, then it was winter,
all surrounded by tall brown grass—even in caper acres,
that winsome nook of tropicalia revolt. Which memories speak
to the future? Nickled, dimed, and quartered. Yet I don't have
any illusions about duration, the slow departure of tendons
from an intricate skeleton; I'm just filing the paperwork,
not filling it out. And if I do my job competently, a peanut
tumbles down the chute after each completed task.

It starts from outside you and ends up outside you.
A chill wind blows off the streets and fields, both dressed
in their best depressed teenager's black, as the shouts
of sanitation workers echo in the street. A polyester lunchbox
washed up on shore, along with stringy kelp, medical syringes,
and enough blinking strobes to induce a seizure. Ears slide
toward the back of the head while leaving the Earth's
atmosphere. Otherwise, help is slow in coming these days,
now that the robot's appendage is crushed in its own machine.
Instead, I recommend the bob-and-weave, or making up names
for travel, because any driver can at least dream of more speed.

Yet any view can later be changed on screen, so I'd begin by
airbrushing out the more prominent stitches and scars.
There's a Pizza Hut on one end of Main Street and a Burger King
on the other. A fairly uneventful afternoon passed in between,
except when a statue of the town's heavily armed founder
was toppled by a bunch of bored kids with a pickup truck and winch.
Confused vultures circled above, unsure if the shards were edible.
A proud nation stood grinning and transfixed, its image beamed
from church to school to chamber-of-commerce breakfast mingler.

Graves come equipped with broken periscopes. Rotting wisteria
clogs the gutters. By seeming coincidence, a different channel
is showing an advertisement for a gutter-hosing device that allows
its user to knock laundry off the line without having to leave
the house. Why do ghosts need clothes, anyway? A wall full
of shiny new toasters reflects a wall full of shiny new toasters,
with a dropped ceiling to close the infinite loop. A barber
with a fresh razor leans in to shave the stubbly skin above
a rapidly pulsing artery.

Trading metaphors for morphine. On a positive note,
one benefit of a flooded hotel room is that it's a short swim
to the self-serve mini-bar, briefly upsetting life's implicit regime
of daily petty humiliations. Need it? I'm ch-ch-choking on it!
Please confirm your contact information, and be sure to provide
an email address as well. Adam's language is strictly nouns.
He shops at Walmart now. Bar codes mostly make sense to him,
as cells continue to divide without ceremony as part
of the newsboy squawk.

What else gets rewarded? Taking a placebo may be the cure,
but the definition of eternity is the wolves are inside the gates.
Cable and phone lines make it easier, but talk about getting
your signals crossed. Stuffed animal trophy kills adorn
a living room wall, with a Vaseline stain on the knitted afghan.
Please remind me again of the club's membership policies,
and let me know if I'll need permission to enter; because
I've been sitting in this same seat for hours, while a helicopter
hovers above, hacking away at a god's bright blue sky.

Meanwhile, the Earth rotates beneath motionless billboards,
and unemployment stands at a ten-year high, as snowdrifts
bury the shovels used to clear them. Stoke a fire in the kitchen,
or at least plug in the microwave—I'm up to my elbows
in dough! A model airplane crashes through a window
while enhanced with digital effects and a swelling soundtrack
that made the flags go stiff in the breeze and neatly fold
themselves up for the night. If you look closely, it appears
as a blur in photographs fading in their frames.

Semis in low gear, skittish sparrows, refrigerator hum.
Lottery balls spill across the set during a live broadcast
drawing to the stunned silence of state officials looking on.
A projectionist steps from behind the curtain, steering wide
of the cape in a slow list, as the crew watches movies
on a slack mainsail while drinking from the sea after freshwater
provisions ran out. But it beats scrubbing capital's bathroom
with a toothbrush and one shredded square of paper towel.
Technology is a parasite passing through glimmering ports.

We're always left to repair the damage afterwards,
as gun-toting skirmishes break out on both sides of the nursery's
gridded glass. Sometimes in a daze, sometimes not. It's more
than a little violence most people endure. Whole towns
were submerged when the river backed up behind the dam.
Downstream went underwater as well, after a streaking satellite
slammed into its towering concrete face, rendering premature
our decision to drain the aquarium and set a place for a guest
who's always late in arriving.

There's a small carbon deposit at the bottom of the heart,
though I don't know what color. Patch a plastic patch
with a plastic patch, or sheepishly emerge from the bushes—
a glowing fluorescent witness, a big glistening paw dipped
in honey. Steel, brick, sky, brick, steel. The distractions
are expected, and the room changes in dimensions whenever
a new occupant enters, with windows more or less opaque
according to the light. Bulldozers plow the orchards
and their uncollected fruit until a choked spring is all that's left
to sift through.

The camera didn't work so good after it got sat on.
Nostalgia is a remembered memory, chewed but not bitten off.
We found ourselves waiting for the undertow when we thought
we were swimming against the tide. Dark days for years.
In what ways is the concept of modern history a European
invention? It clogs love's landfill. Most cities and towns
have only one daily. How many satisfied sidecar occupants?
How many overturned tanker trucks with their gooey gushes?
The DJ pushes play and every emergency room is a dance floor.

Enforcing this is a job for either the Coast Guard or Che Guevara.
The sun sets below an iron-railed promenade, dexterously steering
a 70-mile-per-hour blowout safely curbside. Fuzzy squirrels
and plump-breasted robins crept up to the suburb's edge,
and were frozen in a natural history museum diorama,
along with meteorites, an Emperor penguin, the assassination
of Patrice Lumumba, and a blue whale whose enormous fin
upset a raised tray of martinis at the opening-night fundraising gala
with all the living former presidents in attendance alongside
sundry medicated outpatients.

Turns out the flowers aren't perennials after all. I'm a 15,000-foot
runway, but smaller than a theater. Cabs queue in front of
a train station, where orphans embark for sunnier climes,
sending postcards from Home Depots along the route.
Cardboard boxes get soggy in the rain, or else we eat directly
from the stovetop. It's a race for language on an expected course.
Embedded US reporters didn't offer keener insights into the war,
while hottubbers got down to business after an avalanche
narrowly bypassed the resort, though a nearby forest was flattened
next to an artificial lake that doubles as a watery tomb for rusting
Donner Party skillets.

A black circle on a white background. A mouth agape against
barbed wire. A carpenter slips on a roof while adjusting
an antennae. Images repeat again and again, though the messages
are difficult to discern, broadcast through a megaphone
transmitting from glossy metal to bruised flesh, and leaving
a film behind. How many cameras were set up for one shot?
How many sets destroyed? A baby doesn't smell like a baby
unless it's wearing Pampers. Melting polar icecaps cool
the oceans. There's no such thing as an empty page.

I guess you could say I was born to croon, though I'll keep quiet
if you cut me a check. Go ahead and roll out the deep-fried howitzer;
just make sure the platoon's been fed first, as birds scatter
from a puddle at the cannon's discharge. The ship-salvaging effort
ended up in Walt Disney's rec room, along with a ham-radio operator
codenamed Mercury and a box of radioactive seeds for fighting
prostate cancer. Tonight's network programming consists
primarily of staged reality TV and a scripted press conference.
Objects in mirror are closer than they appear. History yawns,

stretches its arms, and slides across a leather couch to cozy up
with various members of the fraternal order of vicious types.
Sophie and I call them hairy gorillas. Cartoons advertise
last year's model, glinting off the burnished steel of medals
and shells. All we wanted for dinner was taco salad
and the chance to relax after a long day at work, as the pilot
shuts down the plutonium-fueled rockets for a Martian
happy hour rendezvous. After all, isn't it better to be respected
than respectable? A doghouse rests in a cage placed within
a fenced backyard where sweaty evangelists roll over microphones.

Each constellation has an alternate name, an alternate fable,
and an alternate configuration of stars. Every cruise ship toilet
backed up at once, forcing the passengers to wear rubber gloves
to the buffet or captain's table, with drinks mixing anything
alcoholic and free. But who went ahead and changed the locks?
Or shot people in their beds while they slept? Birthday balloons
were sliced ragged by electrical towers after being inadvertently
set loose. Magpies gulped the heliumed slivers, adding an octave
to their calls—from friendship to mating to death sob or wail.

It gives the lie to the law of the jungle and its contested
management. Roads trace the course of rivers and prior trails,
heads bobbing on stacks of vertebrae for the entire trip.
Circling the wagons is inching along in a crowded drive-thru lane
and ordering into a clown's flapping metallic ears, saying,
"This is where the next line goes." Or, your ad here.
Sitcoms are disorienting in a different way; and if expectation
is a vessel, then it's full of holes. So please be patient;
relief comes in a slow drip. A freeway abruptly ended in a desert
where we ate our own skeletons, and then spit them back up
to feed our young.

History is also not a rush for the exits where steeples and minarets
punctuate the rooftops. Heat shimmers off sticky asphalt
next to a foreclosed livestock auction corral. Lightning flashes
against wet grout and low clearance ahead, ignored by a driver
asleep at the wheel in silk underwear bunching to the right.
The robbery transpired in real time, as opposed to the vitrine
in which Bob Marley's soccer cleats are enshrined. Where poetry
tries to swallow it whole, it jams the printer in translation,
with smoke pouring from the front of the machine.

Children were further confused by the drunk crossing guard.
Thankfully, technology came to the rescue with an ingenious device
that combines a breathalyzer with a robotic assistance dog.
It can be further equipped with Hellfire missiles, as can
washing machines, La-Z-Boy recliners, and shopping carts,
which may be why I never saw it coming. No drama, but lots
of characters with eyes x-ed out—less captives of the contemporary
than chained to a forgotten yesterday and a tomorrow
hobbling over on crutches, of time measured in neon blenders
trimming back the branches and leaves before winter sets in.

Long-term patients sleep in the hallways after the beds
were taken by a wayward Boy Scout troupe, compasses aflutter.
The cupboards and drawers had long since been painted shut.
Each morning, a traffic cop tickets a rusting wheelchair chained
to a no parking sign out front, the result of either continental drift
or the more direct infliction of bodily harm. Terns scavenge
the beach next to the minesweepers. A special town hall meeting
was called to discuss the obscure relationship between product
placements in the local nightly news broadcast and a referendum
on ice fishing at the community college hockey rink,

where a Jumbotron-prompted crowd rises to its feet, gnawing
on the carcass of a rotting skunk covered in spit, while waiting
for a busted escalator to be repaired. Is that why the kid's crying?
I'm in low-end retail and gone reflections. There are no secure links,
just photographs of photographs, and everything you can't forget—
sallow streetlights at dusk and again at dawn, because in the span
of four minutes the horizon moves a degree or is launched
into orbit between Earth and Saturn, between death and Florida.
Let's be honest, outer space may be a vacuum, but that orbiting rug
isn't getting any cleaner.

Chickens will soon be bred without inconvenient legs and beaks.
Get me a doctor, Benway. Tires bite into the pavement, as flames
shoot from a tailpipe, not snipers with their hemophiliac dynasty
of Batmans and flight-suit-wearing, chug, chug, banana-boat steering
co-pilots. For lunch, the rest get Triscuits, wine from a box,
and free front teeth extractions. Suddenly, I don't feel so good.
Pictures of puppies donning lopsided bonnets line the walls
of the waiting room. But taking a cold shower on a cold day
makes it worse, spraying rain through an industrial-strength fan
across a stainless steel floor.

Information is a crucial resource, but only streaks on a dare.
First comes a commercial for asteroid-collision insurance
that uses an audio collage of flying saucer melodies for its jingle
and the image of a man trapped behind a large desk, as a person
outside furiously pedals by on a one-speed bike—a speck against
architecture and cirrus clouds. Educated in the finer points
of nothing, that's me at the firing range, shooting myself
in the foot before the first target ever popped up. I swear I heard
the instructor mutter under his breath about sticking to putt-putt,

except for the time I put my club through the 18th hole's raised
and lowered miniature castle drawbridge challenge, as a squadron
of fighter jets screamed overhead. Rocking a car will get it unstuck
faster than spinning its wheels. A supporting actor performs
in front of a bathroom mirror filled with sleeping pills and
allergy medicine in a fabricated public sphere where fake designer
handbags laid out on blankets outsell the real ones displayed in
exclusive boutiques. It's the desert as a mug of spiked fruit punch
for the Saturday night bingo prize; it's the desert as near.

Where is the love? Gone from liars hiding the bodies
under beach blankets. That must also be why the fortune cookies
are empty. I'm going to make some food now and think about
evacuation plans later; as long as I've got a couple rolls
of Scotch tape and Saran Wrap, I should be okay until the mist
disperses. Besides, the traffic leaving the city late on a Friday
is just insane. Yet there's always a new rollercoaster claiming
to be the fastest or to have the most 360s. At this point,
feel free to boo the villain. He's not the one fiendishly twisting
his moustache; no, that's the bearded lady circus performer.
She's cool.

Some rims keep spinning after the tires have stopped,
chipping away at space-time continuums. Power is ambient
when it's not really loud, because there's no such thing
as pure noise. And another thing: the room service is terrible here!
Um, there isn't any room service. Well, no wonder it's so bad!
The border patrol crouches in bushes beneath the window,
but there's no one nibbling at the electrical cord except us
rabbits and a happy, happy cicada whose click and whir
gave us away to the authorities. Thanks a lot, little cicada.
Or maybe we're in a getaway car patiently waiting for the light
to turn green.

But that's only a small corner of the picture, with the bosses
in the audience and the doors blocked with crossed halberds.
The walls and towers do fall. A newborn listens to the swoosh
of blood through a mother's heart. An entire military band
was replaced by a sampler. A cargo ship waits to be filled
with sugar after pumping out its oil, where beef is stacked
next to Nikes on an automated dock. Where are the criminals
in a wolfpack? Preying on those most vulnerable during
the dry season and its same bucket of dirty water used
for bathing, drinking, and washing clothes.

Arriving planes vanish into the smog and reappear at the gate.
The airport Marriott hosts an annual stowaways convention.
My parents retired a few years ago, but memory doesn't wipe
its feet at the door. Besides, this isn't *The Jetsons,* even though
I was told the future is now, and the present either starves you
to death or eats you alive. Many more people are killed each year
by lightning strikes than shark attacks, which doesn't include
statistics on spontaneous combustion, the mysteries of sweet meats,
marauding fermented pear eaters, and official timekeepers
from somewhere between love it here and stuck here.

In any case, there's no starting over, no symmetry to loss.
We pack our one-way ticket to a ghost town, with Charlton Heston
intoning on the audio tour, as images flash by in a digital slideshow
seen through tinted windows, and pupils dilate in the gloaming
with its insomnia of muskets, water cannons, and smokestacks
framing a lunar eclipse. Now it's nearing last call, followed by
closing time's unforgiving blotchy skin. A jumble of empties
sways precariously in the sink, while ashes and dollar bills
collect on the bar.

Contents under pressure. Zoo animals used a series of seesaws
to escape from their enclosures, but I'm not going to invent
a story for this, since every history has a history. A refrigerated rack
of pre-packaged cold cuts yearns to meet a pile of coupons
bound with a paperclip. The whole town used to cheer when
the circus arrived. Carcinogens collect in animal fat carved
into nearly opaque opera glasses pressed against sunken eyes
and smashed archives. A cracked compact and pine tree-shaped
air freshener rattle in a racecar's glove compartment while
tow trucks stand ready at the finish line to haul away the debris.
The world is buried in time—

drop by drop. But it doesn't always add up. Cops kick in the door
to the wrong apartment. Even spiders got into the act, weaving
a range of anti-pastoral aspersions into their drooping barnyard webs.
Mollusks cling to the sleek hull of a somersaulting powerboat
and its advertisements blurry from shore. Impatient fans attacked
the team's mascot during an endless rain delay, and so were given
free hayrides from the parking lot to the mall, from the deepest
unassisted freedive to the cigarette machine. A sword swallower's act
was updated for the nuclear age, as spectators bask in its luster,
wearing lead tank tops on casual Fridays at the office.

Investigators wade through the wreckage and its tumbling logic.
Sound waves quickly rippled from a sonic boom that startles
dog show contestants and brought a juggler's act to a swift conclusion
with meat cleaver, postage stamp, and the Apollo 17 nosecone
crashing to the floor. Those price tags go on those rodeos,
go on those epaulets. Buses leave every fifteen minutes
during rush hour, but get stuck behind meticulous lane painters
holding a canned food drive. Gravediggers try not to think about it
too much, all those blades of grass harboring reincarnation.

Small bonfires flare up from the cutting-room floor, where
the frames are etched in red with satellite-pinpointed dates
and places. The blank time in between ended up on greeting cards
and a dashboard's sun-bleached promissory notes. Dry leaves
blow clear of bare limbs, with Mars and Venus flickering low
on the horizon in a corporate logo. The cheese should be plenty ripe
by now, as a dump truck eases back and expels its load of cinders
and pelts. Diesel fumes billow through a canary's cage built
by field mice and salt harvesters near the ocean.

A map is accurate in how many dimensions? A crew of ragpickers
found discarded *Wheel of Fortune* letters in a dumpster behind
the studio amid egg salad and makeup. Flakes of skin drift
through a sunbeam and frequencies embedded within frequencies,
like in a blissed-out game of musical chairs in which wobbling sirens
blend with scraps of nursery rhymes and glass bottles smashed
against walls. A riverbed glistens with small stones; at its edge,
a pile of shoes and socks props open the door of our passing,
as virtual lungs stammer their breath into each street, every season.

PRETTY WORDS MADE A FOOL
OUT OF ME

A crowd of witnesses gathers
in front of a brick wall covered
with mayonnaise to which no

picture stays affixed for long,
but is another stone added
to a burnt cairn. Pink tanks

find camouflage beneath piles
of prom dresses, as the
wallflowers are wallpapered

with three kinds of meats. There
are even rules for misbehaving
and its inheritance of carpet

showroom flagship store dynasties,
with their executive class
wardrobe of velour track suit

and thong. Instead, we get a
palace full of hack journalists—
every desk supplied with nontoxic

glue, masking tape, and coffee-
ringed coordinates, like drawing
an X over each page of a foldout

map used to make house calls
on the 4th of July. A swarm
of imperial butterflies snuffs

out a tree lamp while the dinner
guests politely ignore a putrid
mastodon at the table, with cigar-

chomping political ambitions
and millennia of matted hair
lifted straight from permafrost,

and semi-opaque plastic and glass
beads covering the throne. A
nation beyond 17 acres and its

ragged banners and souvenirs soaks
the sand with blood to make kitchen
sponges. A Coney Island knife

thrower with an underhand fast-
pitch softball motion slings
cleavers into the ocean. Here go

the bridges burning one by one,
as each present life becomes
a former life, and there's not

enough yellow tape in the entire
world to cordon off that crime
scene. A shopping cart smashes

through the windshield of an
ambulance speeding to the wreck.
Security was again tight for the

home and garden show, with
a sniper on every rooftop and
helicopters buzzing the crowd.

Preferred buyers go to the front
of the line, though there's a line
for that line, too. Cremated remains

rest in a Folgers coffee can on the
mantle, squeezing the light from it.
The without is within, opening

the cabin door for spring to hear
the noisy geometry of landing
planes powered by a captain

propelled by sugar. I learned
most of what I know about
classical music from Disney.

A child sings a nursery rhyme
into a digital tornado flinging
livestock, tractors, and Henry

Kissinger's international canceled
stamp collection at the imaginary
camera. Then nothing. Then

nothing again. Or else the technology
of war. Patches of snow, rockets
march in a Beetle Bailey goosestep

parade and dirty bathwater. I is woven
in, lips and tongues caked with salt,
while gnawing on monuments and

their real-time Prussian and vicar
images eroded by rain and acidic
pigeon shit. A spotlight scans

the food court at the mall where
a skewered pig rotates over an open
fire next to a children's play area

with its stained gray carpet and
little hands on parents' soft leather
shoes that smell like fried onions,

like decaying bats. Blueberry
blossoms float in a bog above
discarded tires and a mattress.

Crows won't abandon their carrion
outlined in neon far beneath
the rustle of whatever destroys us

and its dark wings at 30,000 feet,
because flightless birds don't
symbolize flight, those rubber

penguin beaks served up as art
at the home team's free-trade
clambake. A dental drill rattles

the fillings loose, leaving tiny
holes in speech, like the cracks
in mortar doctors apply to stigmatas.

Duck and cover won't save us;
neither will a god. Hairy-knuckled
tribes push hard on the throttle

and raze villages in Dolby sound
and Bose speakers. Poetry's voice
is broken; don't fix it. Can I tell

you about our specials? Tonight
we have fruit salad on paper plates
in a slow line of fingerprinting—

facts sliding into fictions, fictions
sliding into facts. Here comes another
set of commercials. I gotta get paid

in hair and food clogging Babylon's
drain. It makes sense for a while,
following a chain of command

wrapped in layers of ambient noise,
of rhetoric propping up reality
stuffed with antebellum cotton

and hay, and linked to an atomic
clock. What's the vocabulary for
this? What's the frequency, Kenneth,

for safe passage? You sat on a star
and had your sunglasses crushed.
The bosses land in a spaceship

to pick up the pieces. There was
also the time a 400-lb Andean
hummingbird chipped off parts of

the hillside Hollywood sign looking
for nectar and an expectorant.
A fire escape doubles as an iron

garden where the trees were late
in blooming against a prerecorded
landscape of beer cans and landmines.

Mi casa es tu casa. Wheel spokes
pass in a blur of kids' bikes
pedaled to swim team practice,

to dad's annual Memorial Day
bear hunt. The pelts turned up
at the local trading post with its

assortment of moisturizers and
log-rolling competition trophies.
Flesh grows over disused cave

pool eyes, as the wind helps shape
the form and saws through
the defenses. At the end of the day,

all the toys were put in a box and
the lid snapped shut. An Exxon
blimp floated above the Super Bowl

halftime show, dropping a rope
ladder to the last line dancer, as
fans circled the bright concession

area concourse and its backdrop
of war rations and skin grafts.
This is a test of the emergency

alert system. Afterward, air traffic
controllers returned to their cloud-
limned daydreams, brown incense

stick ashes dropping on the console.
A gun pokes into the edge of the
frame, and is lost amid a thicket

of palm trees, glitter, hearts, and
various types of personal weapons.
Then the parachute failed to open,

but that's okay because the fall
was less than 10 feet, dragging
each other through a mud we go

out of our way to locate, and can't
just stand up and dust off like
the animals that only see in infrared.

Instead, we're stunned by the sudden
appearance of oncoming headlights,
of incoming wounded, as power

always finds an outlet, ingesting
sitcom camaraderie and robotic
cockfights. That's why prisoners

plot their escape. The turnips in
the painting look good enough
to paint. But it's back to rainy days

and election years. I guess you
could call them memories, gobbling
up the neo-burlesque floorboards.

Nearby, the pipeline project was
extended with insulated work gloves,
solid steel hammers, and a smudgy

wink. What's on TV right now?
These monuments are built to be
destroyed. Someone cast a spell on

the Thanksgiving turkey. Language
can sometimes work like that,
swirling with credit card receipts

and skipping along chains of
desire and nutritional supplements
in full view of blue against blue,

but pixels break up when they're
enlarged too much. Within a
week, all the trees were in full

bloom. Police cars race down a
scrolling videogame street. Common
courtesy suggests keeping a camel

with the runs away from an oasis.
The explosions were virtually
inserted. I'd have had a better

view if I'd looked into the correct
end of the telescope. And taken
the lens cap off. And removed

my blindfold. Because an inverted
reality TV show is still a reality
TV show, i.e., truth is a different

kind of embellishment, making
the jump to the big screen, all
blond hair and beefcake abs,

as the audience chews through
rows of fluffy white pancakes.
I left my plastic fork at the rodeo

where we eat with our hands,
and later curl up together
like an S or a question mark.

Thousands of eligible voters
were purged from the rolls. A
favorite pet lost patches of hair

after rolling around on a freshly
fertilized lawn. Poppy is a more
lucrative cash crop than wheat,

than the soft heads of tulips nodding
close to a sharp blade taken from
'70s kung fu movies with their

carefully constructed social orders
and an umpire squatting low behind
the plate. How much do they charge

for that? Fargo's marshmallow-
filled sandbags ride floodwaters
with Mississippi's leaky coffins,

with the violence families teach.
I need another cup of coffee
and some creamer. I need advice.

Renting a forklift wasn't necessary
to take out the trash, spilling pudding
and bundles of struck matches.

Cameras were on the spot to
document one of those mirrored-
sunglasses-beneath-baseball-cap-

pulled-low-and-hair-in-a-ponytail
celebrity sightings. A cacophony
of bird songs fills the neighborhood's

sole living tree. We spent parts
of the day submerged in the animal
chamber, then watched ticklish

starfish in a tidal pool mottled with
oil slicks and gray lottery ticket
scratchings. Generators buzz loudly

in the night with its occupying
armies fighting their wars at home.
The next day, everyone was an

orphan. Free hot air balloon rides
didn't change anything, except
the distance to both the sea and

the mop next to the sink. All my
years of service to this company,
and I still can't tell time. Otherwise,

it's loss by accretion, bare thighs
squeaking friction on a playground
slide. I wrote it all down in a letter,

which I didn't write and never
sent. There's no limit to what
you can win. The Kool-Aid man

crashed through brick walls to
reach the thirsty children. Straws
sprouted where each jagged

piece of glass fell. Water kept
the kidneys flushed, as ice
sculptures made from antifreeze

drip onto Halliburton's free lunch
buffet, shattering the illusion of
professional knowledge and its

hired mercenaries. Wolves huddle
against a cold rain gobbling up room
on a hard drive. Even the butterflies

were armed, their pollen collectors
sensitized to hunger. Television sets
end a thousand silences, and poems

fold into their antennas. Meanwhile,
I spin my knobby wheels in an all-terrain
vehicle purchased with discarded

fish sticks. A kite pushed in a shopping
cart flies horizontally. Tom Cruise
ready for love again. Duration is a

performance, a backyard wrestling
ring strewn with upturned thumbtacks.
I came down the assembly line

pushing each day's needle into
a corkboard mowed to the edge
of a sodded igloo. Marmosets

chattered in the trees, as tractor
mutilation stories softly played
in the lobby. The horizon line tilts

toward Monday and its discarded
plastic shopping bags collecting
against a chain-link fence. Sleet fell

through holes in the roof, heads
resting on dirty pillows with their
faded MADE IN USA labels. It also

rhymes with bacon, with Operation
Rolling Thunder, because language
goes on without me, but not without you.

Still, it's feeling cramped in this box
called tomorrow with its four sharp
edges and rounded letters. I ate

a sandwich for lunch, then worked
on my screenplay about driving
a fire truck to the nearest Ice Age.

Soldiers returning from war
surprise adjectives, like flags
made from lasagna after austerity

measures left needle and thread
in short supply. Every image seeks
its caption. What industries support

this town? We make dolls without
addresses, and invent new uses
for landfills. The celebrity's driver

became a celebrity, but not the driver's
mechanic or the travel plaza gas pump
attendant with binoculars sweeping

the desert for UFOs and Cadillacs,
for Nixon and hippies. These highways
empty into the sea. The sea empties

into lungs. Lungs empty into dust—
a fly trapped between panes of
glass. The day quickly reverts to

default mode. The candidate's
pitch was very convincing, although
I said hi before I realized it was

a recording putting the lid down
on toilet bowls and seen eclipses.
Then I hobbled back to my day

job of fits and starts, of waiting
in Payless for the other shoe to
drop. I don't know if it's mine or

not. I'm not even following this,
except in aprons and wetsuits.
It was a cold night along the

marathon route and its booths
set up for screen tests. Tanks
splinter palm trees into mess hall

toothpicks gathered by refugees,
as descending helicopters churn a
fish pond and hand-dug well near

one small pair of socks for every
child killed in the bombing. All
the colors were changed on the

digital foliage. Even the Death Star
became a vacation destination,
with blinds drawn after the desert

slowed down its breathing. Boys race
to a swimming pool behind McDonald's,
as stores stay open during the holiday,

selling stuffed blouses for the
next top model search. A solitary
teenager collects empty shopping carts

in a parking lot, because buying in
bulk is usually cheaper, whether
chewed cuticles or distressed jeans.

Satellites take photos of gardeners
and clear vinyl covers on living room
couches, where the dye stays but fades,

like Cary Grant riding a crumpled Vespa,
or the way you tilt the sky behind me.
Lapping water tends to the rushes.

Candles burn down to their holders,
dripping wax on arsonist wigs,
Sunday hams, and the sour cream

that won in a taste test. There's much
to be agitated about in a stadium full
of mirrors collecting TV static

and a run on the banks with
other go-kart drivers. Stray dogs
swim in the moat. It's convenient

to eat while shopping, where the
King of Sex meets the Onion King.
What's lost in lawn-mowing

accuracy is made up for in speed
or Astroturf. Biography is its own
form of fiction, but sometimes

there's a wound so deep everything
threatens to fall in it. I mean,
what's the point in visiting

the emergency room now? So put
away that portable cooking stove.
From here on out, it's reconnaissance

missions using clay pigeons, followed
by a Sherpa complex or tailspin
à la mode, because the sun sets on

whatever isn't perpetually airborne,
which is fine by me. I think of
the future in my daughter's tiny

heart. I think of the future of the
future. A police van in an alley
sits quietly with its lights off.

Shoe tips poke out from behind
a curtain. You can have the leg,
but please don't take the cane.

Conveyer belts move items closer
to the register. Robots don't know
when they perform the robot dance,

stepping on metal feet but adverse
to tire swings over rising tides.
I guess it depends on the degree

of the sugar bowl's slope, as you push
while I'm pulling on the rudder.
A few houses survived the storm,

all the damage surveyed from the top
of a footstool beginning with the letter a.
Garbage cans roll around in the street.

For its big night out, memory went heavy
on the rouge. Geologists map avalanches
for oil and sand traps, as cheerleaders

cheer on cheering, and the viewers
lick spackle from the walls after
greasing wagon trains with butter

and spandex. A flock of birds
moves on and off the screen, just as
there's a big thing crawling on me.

Cold air rushes through the heating
vents of Tom Brokaw's convertible
and tray full of burgers and methane.

Send in the clones. Those lovable
clones. Alien abductions seem to occur
only in a few countries. Then I'm back

to staring at walls and sunlight
filtering through the blinds, or
tucking blankets neatly piled on

Walmart's loading dock and scratching
where a scar used to be. Yet somewhere
there's a harvest. Three of the wheels

were missing hubcaps made into
sluggish wind chimes as sound
flakes from analog, from lace collars

and guillotines. A mammal caught
by its tale still has a chance to escape
and sew up the patient. Meals are

an assemblage of smaller pieces,
just as information eats its words.
Flags are planted in the tops of skulls,

but there's no perimeter to secure, sir—
just a green room with B-list game
show hosts and porn actresses eating

complimentary pretzels. Cells battle
radioactive orchards scorched brown
by frost. The review declared it:

Sunny and reassuring . . . with beguiling
pictures. Submerged chuck wagons tickled
by shrimp legs attract sharks trailing

ships of state turning lifeboats into
gunboats. No wonder there are
people who don't want to go home.

Speed is addictive in a culture
of assault where the police break
the law to enforce it. A forklift

wobbles with its load, as stray
cats sprint for cover in an empty
parking garage built over a drained

coral reef. It's also where the
neighborhood kids play. Some
have had a parent die or move

away or were stalled out on the launch
pad by mission control. Not so,
the can-do squadron commanders

rousing the troops for an early
morning jog and cigarette. Who
says the sky is falling? Cars wait

patiently in line at a railroad crossing.
Then less patiently. Boil the noodles
until tender. Superheroes start with

stick figures, as you face a forest fire
with a handful of sand and your
halo down around your ankles.

That's why we're preoccupied
with love. Big spaceships give birth
to little spaceships, each designed

for an initial struggle with gravity and
snowmobilers carrying concealed
weapons. Hearing aids drop out of

lunchboxes packed for everyday
life's din of broken transmissions,
but if you told me everything I don't know,

I'd listen to you forever. The mandated
distance between commercial jets
decreases. The book's spine stayed

mostly intact, while the seasons
changed without us. The road isn't
a metaphor—it's just a road. I

stitched my arm into a curtain
I thought to pull back with its
standing order for the politics

of vaudeville. Puppet heads peer
through rat traps and tinted windows,
the drivers talking to themselves

during the trip, as cartographers begin
to go out of business in the rhomboid
shadows of bus tours and armored

convoys. Through it all, well-wishers
gathered outside the courthouse,
sporadically setting off the metal

detectors used after hours to irradiate
piles of expired meat. Astronauts
train beneath the sea in lead boots

and corduroy. The experiment involves
incubators wheeled out of closets
and TVs hanging precariously from

the walls, while wet letters dry on the
windowsills. The legible is transient,
which is far from starting over.

BYE-BYE, BIG WOW

PULLEY SYSTEM

I'm switching the channel now, so please
leave the historical monuments at home
and bring the pesticide toothpaste instead.
Language toys with seduction where
it leaks from the bottom each time the day
speaks of blindness, gnaws on the same
patch of sidewalk, terminal damage.
What does a snowman need with an electric
ice cream maker while waving an inverted
broom at the difference in the same?

Of course the jaws of life are dangerous.
What color is love? We sleep on sirens.
We are the dog tags on our neighbor
released from a clenched fist, spent on
TV, and given presents like two giants
wrestling. On the shadow puppets' small
stage, two drunks punched each other.
My head hurt from swallowing a gold cup.

That's why I always wanted to serve on
a pirate ship. You told me you hid the keys
beneath the sink. I said possession,
and couldn't stop thinking of the lake
drained to build shiny below-ground condos.
Try to be more cheerful. I smell the bathroom
from the hall. Yes, you did already mention
the hummingbird in the Sansabelt pants
commercial. What can you really know
alone?

BUDDY SYSTEM

Farewell, heroics on high school athletic
fields. Hello, sod farm. Hello, children
of divorce. There's no ice queen with
peeling tooth enamel, just a canary that lost
its favorite chew toy under the slightly
sinister porch, a helicopter-aided caribou
migration, a war fought for the sake of
an idea on the back of a playbill.

I've never been sure of the way to end
or begin a poem. The cancer was vigorously
attacked with a series of treatments,
then all the flags were licked and stuck on
car windows as temporary stickers,
while seaborne container ships plow
fields of protein.

I've accrued enough miles to fly to the
Middle East for free. When you think of
engineering, please envision desalination
plants and their patinated love affairs with
algae. A system can only withstand so much
disequilibrium before it collapses into stasis.
The crook of your arm presses against
my neck. Now. Here. Meaning: there.

MULTIPLE SERVING SIZE

Yellow lines shield the pedestrians from
the cars, the platforms from the subways,
as the gradual glow of a new day with its
you-really-no-you-really-shouldn't-have
fruit baskets makes the rounds of outpatient
visits. It's called hope by another name.
It's still quiet on the porn shoot set. Clear-
cutting eroded the soil past the horizon,
like pounding a bank teller's glass with
phantom limbs later lost in the machine.

After all that, now it's time for band
practice? Crap. Computers and humans fall
asleep in the same room, because home
is imagined. A blind taste test compared
microwavable quiche and skiwear. The bird
metaphors read differently in the wake of
avian flu and monogamous penguins living
mostly separate lives. Images can be incorrectly
assigned.

Nevertheless, it requires a large window
to view the entire length of the intestines in
a single sitting. What's the downloadable
ringtone for virtual pneumatics, for hunters
and gatherers with strobe lights? Some
winters are colder than others, however cozy
the cuffs and collars monogrammed in red
with the initials EAT. Delivery drivers riding
scooters are creative with their routes beneath
supermarket billboards advertising envelopes
and honey.

LOW CLEARANCE AHEAD

For security purposes, all visitors must
sign in first and check any oily rags
at the windowsill. For more information
regarding the domestic symptoms of
social crisis, please visit a self-service
kiosk. It's different from a boy band
doing its own Disneyland sound check,
from scraping an internal parasite with
a rusty razor tossed in the day's dented
trashcan.

I'm sorry, I meant to say a bad hair day,
a defenestration, when what you asked for
was a moment of silence, and received a
chainsaw in your ear tasting like a mixture
of sugar, diabetes, and love. Instead, listen
to what your friend tells you, such as:
an obsessive thinks with the hands, touching
fine faultlines in the surrounding surfaces,
or having teeth removed in order to better
hum this tune.

Storm clouds remake the sky into the color
of a bruise, though it took a long time for
rain to actually fall. Pain is not an initiation
but a system, made sad in reverse. People
and animals sought shelter and stutter
under the bridges crossed by satellites,
while small boats and swimmers were forced
to evacuate the lake, all that possibility
turning impossible in the mirror factory.

HOLY ROLLERS

It's the time of exile. Even the dogs
have abandoned the table. There are
new navigators, gleaming new hinges
on the bomb bay doors, a sewn flashlight
squeezing dubbed hangover balloons.
Call it the militarization of everyday life
where not all voices are public—
a history glossing the good son's
desperate call from the tarmac.

The howling started in the backyard,
then gradually moved inside. That's
when I threw a TV at it, like collapsing
an air pocket in an avalanche. Cool
hunters inspected the damage and
attached tracking devices that functioned
beneath polar ice caps. Just so you know,
let it go means a part of me goes with it
at the America's Cup of flashing steak
knives.

The light switch is outside the bathroom.
I don't give a damn how people are
expected to have sex. To me, the most
frightening law of all is maximize profit.
And while it may appear that we're
alone, you're forgetting about the hungry
ghosts and benign ham eaters quietly
chewing in the kitchen. Boysenberries
rot in pools of rainwater. No one hedges
their bets when the only outcome is loss.

THE DEVIL IS IN THE DETAILS

Those were happier times, though they
didn't seem so happy then, like a dark
river glimpsed in the corner of a mouth.
Now it's all moving faster in a harsh
brightness, replacing neon for sand
in the pulley system weights. Be careful,
that gun fires blanks on Wall Street—
the stars & stripes of casual sex.

Rescue helicopters crash on their way
back to the hospital for regular skull
injections and hip replacements. I don't
presume to understand how it all works.
Obey the small rules and break the big
ones. Your ceramic ashtray cast two
shadows in a parking lot overlooking
the port.

I went to the doctor's office to read
the waiting room's neat stack of women's
magazines for divorcees. You went
because you knew something was wrong.
You were right, if getting dripped on by
a banking plane's air conditioner is any
solace. Is there a metaphysics of pain?
Of recent images? God shits through rows
of squeezed paint tubes. God shits on
my hands.

Honor system

You didn't say about another person:
"Maybe they'll be okay." So where's the line
between choice and submission? I get
the message, though I'm not sure which
one. It's not like we didn't lose consciousness
midway through the elaborate filing procedure.
I woke up with my chest dented near a
heavy metal drawer. You spread fresh hay
on the roof for the donkey somnambulist,
the soaking dream's blood stain.

Put money in the jar to pay for copies. Find
the runaway. Even the stomach is conditioned
by culture and sat on by the heart when its
arms grow tired of holding itself up. Rows
of storefronts line a street of near-imperceptible
hollows and security guards paid by the hour.
The wheels of an overturned tractor trailer spin
slower and slower, a brief moment of liberation
for cold sores and cautious skeet shooters.

The challenge, then, is to minimize injury
to innocent bystanders, because they have
their own set of witnesses to care for. There
are popular TV shows to keep up with,
glistening bacon strips to accidentally drip
on freshly knitted quilts. Junior arsonists
practice on books of matches. Junior bowlers
use plastic pins. Desire is a metaphor;
a raised weapon is real.

LISTENING DEVICE

We build a shelter from abandoned tires
and roll it toward the animal preserve,
as a monorail and its swaying snack car
whiz by overhead. First the legroom
is removed, then the legs. I think the
DVD player cost less than $40, plus
shipping. Ingested calipers couldn't
measure the infections in tatters, the
disposable serving trays awkwardly
run over.

Carry-on luggage slouches at the curb.
Every reflection is distorted in binoculars
waved at the stars from sea, from the
mall's parking lot and puddles. Why
should the prey love the predator? I'll
admit to stealing office supplies and a
wrinkled rag stuffed in the gas tank after
the cap got misplaced in the dark night
of America's bloated stillbirth.

Is it easier or more difficult to leave now?
Or to learn to be a foreigner in the land
in which you were born? Thumbs find
their own link on a chain, while the ghost
heads and synthesizer folk are passed
back and forth at the family reunion.
There's no turning the sound down,
however quiet the hour. Borrowed time
confuses the crossing guard.

SLIPPERY SLOPE

In the land of the very large shopping
carts, a horse's grave costs almost nothing,
and teeth chip on the crest of each
unmarked speed bump. How many prints
can be made from the same negative?
Which bridges were shelled from a
distance? Tissue samples are easily
replaced in a time when everything
is taken away except a different time.

Sudden rains cleared days of heat, left
the descending figures to their beds.
The heart is a document. Blood clots
an incision and Lascaux bibs flapping
with tongues in the jet stream. Besides,
there's no such thing as is. Florescent office
and store lights stayed on during nights spent
working on a wrecking ball's mechanics.

Tragedy is a question of the law, where
the son stares on dumbly. Then the places
changed their names. No wonder you felt
better after throwing up all that seasoned
lump meat and spoiled mortar. Crows
wrap the rest in aluminum foil for the
stagger home. It's always either too much
or not enough. Hard surfaces are haunted
by makeshift aqualungs. So what's a
swimming hole?

STILL LIFE

It's difficult to light a signal fire when
all the matches are underwater, like
being talked down from a ledge in the
basement, in the upper playground.
The main concern is that the children
get out safely. Afterward, it's stop,
drop, and roll during the phased reentry
of lunar modules, during the gradual
acclimation of iron mallets and design.

Language carves a space from flesh,
drinks from hard architecture—my
bucket where dogs wash their muddy jaws.
We're out of blankets again. It's the late
afternoon as scatter. Cops stretch their leather
leggings and monitor responses. Mouthfuls
of junk push needles through cotton sleeves.
I'd trade it all for a chance to crash test
aerial minesweepers.

I'm unclear whether it's Santa Claus
or a spacesuit full of edible clay. Traffic
backed up for miles to watch time move
slowly and the desert shift an inch.
A friend imagined Abraham Lincoln as less
hirsute, even at close range. I knew you
were going on a tour of the craters,
but it was a shock to discover a coffin
of empty spoons left behind.

PARTY PLATTER VERSUS EPICURE

Steam rises from an opened dishwasher's
rows of artificial arms and soggy sandpaper.
All the safety latches went missing, as we
held our breath with each water landing.
There were no fresh starts, only already
broken parts broken off, like, Where are you
going? Or a bit too enthusiastically tied
to the railroad tracks with a villain nowhere
in sight.

A dashboard full of sun-softened plastic
saints drives through a carwash on the way
to a pharmacist prescribing a medicine cabinet
for the lap and lost belief in the father.
Sometimes the cure is worse than the illness.
Otherwise, you learn to adapt to the rolling
blackouts, the memories limbs harbor, the
matching latex hat and pin—whether courtier
or courtesan.

Although it's January, it's never too early
to begin thinking about that next lawnmower
purchase. Competitive financing is available,
and you don't even need a lawn. Dusk settled
over the bakery first. Who paid to have another
layer of white paint applied to the walls?
Repair crews lower a metal plate onto
a power line fallen in the road; we added
butter and eggs, inhaling the tires' slowly
severing treads.

COMPLETE GUIDE TO SERVING

Bad news scattered the tourists with their
portable drafting boards covered in snow.
Who put the crown in a skillet with doo-doo
fixings? Weapons are stored in the pantry,
though sometimes our rage makes us silent,
a blindfold for the mouth. After an illustrious
career, I now perform for drink tickets at
Saturday matinees. A whole town of people
sleep in their cars, bound and broken and
choking on asphalt. During the holidays,
collect calls pour in from upstate.

We were excited to see a real forklift
unfasten the moon from the night. Fingers
press temporary fillings into plastic teeth
and stitch wool blankets to bathing suits.
Begin with relation, splintered crutches
and all, kicked out by childhood. I don't
know what happened, though I later found
a syringe and half-eaten chicken wing under
the dentist's chair. The shape of memory
is the shape of desire. The soup took a long
time to cool.

Dirty weather undid predictions and shivered
the candy wrappers' small pollen bells. Then
the staff confiscated all the sharps, making up
laws on the spot. The cookbook was stained
with food more than it's used, because hunger
is its own form of consumption. The seasons

changed while we drove in circles.

                                   There it goes.

Watch it fade away with nowhere to go.

                                        The

zookeeper's glass eye rolled into the monkey
cage, where backs and bellies bend around flags
of soldered straw.

ACKNOWLEDGEMENTS

The poem "Relative Heat Index" appeared in a different version in *Free Radicals: American Poets Before Their First Books*, edited by Jordan Davis and Sarah Manguso (Honolulu/Oakland/New York: Subpress, 2004).

Excerpts from "Pretty Words Made a Fool Out of Me" appeared in *The Canary, Jacket,* and *mark(s)*.

Poems from "Bye-bye, Big Wow" appeared in *Mandorla, The Believer, PoetryPolitic: A Blog in 50 Days,* and *Tarpaulin Sky*.

SplitLevel Texts would like to thank Alan Gilbert for his work, and for the care with which he engaged the editing process. We would also like to thank MPublishing for its support. This book would not have been possible in the absence of either.

ALAN GILBERT

Alan Gilbert is the author of the poetry book, *Late in the Antenna Fields* (Futurepoem), and a collection of essays, articles, and reviews entitled *Another Future: Poetry and Art in a Postmodern Twilight* (Wesleyan University Press). His poems have appeared in *The Baffler, BOMB, Boston Review, Chicago Review, Denver Quarterly, Fence, jubilat,* and *The Nation,* among other places. His writings on poetry and art have appeared in a variety of publications, including *Aperture, Artforum, The Believer, Bookforum, Cabinet, Modern Painters, Parkett,* and *The Village Voice.* He has contributed art catalogue essays and entries for a number of biennials, group shows, and solo exhibitions. He's the recipient of a 2009 New York Foundation for the Arts Fellowship in Poetry and a 2006 Creative Capital Foundation Award for Innovative Literature. He lives in Brooklyn.